First World War
and Army of Occupation
War Diary
France, Belgium and Germany

52 DIVISION
Divisional Troops
Divisional Ammunition Column
1 April 1918 - 31 May 1919

WO95/2892/5

The Naval & Military Press Ltd
www.nmarchive.com
Published in association with The National Archives

Published by

The Naval & Military Press Ltd

Unit 10 Ridgewood Industrial Park,

Uckfield, East Sussex,

TN22 5QE England

Tel: +44 (0) 1825 749494

www.naval-military-press.com

www.nmarchive.com

This diary has been reprinted in facsimile from the original. Any imperfections are inevitably reproduced and the quality may fall short of modern type and cartographic standards.

© **Crown Copyright**
Images reproduced by permission of The National Archives, London, England, 2015.

Contents

Document type	Place/Title	Date From	Date To
Heading	WO95/2892/5 Divisional Ammunition Company		
Heading	52nd Division 52nd Divl Ammunition Col. Apr 1918-May 1919		
Heading	52nd Divisional Artillery Disembarked Marseilles From Egypt 12.4.18. 52nd Divisional Ammunition Column R.F.A. April 1918		
War Diary	Moascar	01/04/1918	02/04/1918
War Diary	Alexandria	03/04/1918	03/04/1918
War Diary	At Sea	04/04/1918	11/04/1918
War Diary	Marseilles	12/04/1918	13/04/1918
War Diary	Train	14/04/1918	15/04/1918
War Diary	Noyelles	16/04/1918	16/04/1918
War Diary	Port Le Grand	17/04/1918	30/04/1918
Heading	War Diary Of 52nd Divisional Ammn Col. From 1.5.1918 To 31.5.18 Vol III		
War Diary	Embry	01/05/1918	01/05/1918
War Diary	Crequy	02/05/1918	07/05/1918
War Diary	Sautrecourt	08/05/1918	14/05/1918
War Diary	Magnicourt	15/05/1918	15/05/1918
War Diary	Estree Cauchie	16/05/1918	22/05/1918
War Diary	Villers Au Bois	23/05/1918	31/05/1918
Heading	War Diary Of 52nd Div Amm. Col. From 1 June 1918 To 30 June 1918 Volume 4		
War Diary	Villers Au Bois	01/06/1918	04/06/1918
War Diary	Mt St Eloi	05/06/1918	30/06/1918
Heading	War Diary Of 52nd Divisional Ammunition Column From 1.7.18 To 31.7.18 (Volume VII)		
War Diary	Mt St Eloi	01/07/1918	20/07/1918
War Diary	Ourton	21/07/1918	29/07/1918
War Diary	Madagascar Camp	30/07/1918	31/07/1918
Heading	War Diary Of 52nd Divisional Ammunition Column From 1st August 1918 To 31st August 1918 Vol VIII.		
War Diary	Habarcq	01/08/1918	01/08/1918
War Diary	Maroeuil	02/08/1918	14/08/1918
War Diary	Frevin Capelle	15/08/1918	20/08/1918
War Diary	Monchiet	21/08/1918	21/08/1918
War Diary	Grosville	22/08/1918	27/08/1918
War Diary	Nr Mercatel	28/08/1918	31/08/1918
Heading	War Diary Of 52nd Divisional Ammunition Column From 1-9-1918 To 30-9-1918 (Volume IX)		
War Diary	Near Mercatel	01/09/1918	01/09/1918
War Diary	Near Henin	02/09/1918	02/09/1918
War Diary	Near Cagnicourt	03/09/1918	08/09/1918
War Diary	Near Croisilles	09/09/1918	21/09/1918
War Diary	Near Lagnicourt	22/09/1918	26/09/1918
War Diary	Louverval	27/09/1918	27/09/1918
War Diary	Near Moeuvres	28/09/1918	28/09/1918
War Diary	Near Graincourt	29/09/1918	30/09/1918
Heading	War Diary Of 52nd Divisional Ammunition Column From 1-10-18 To 31-10-18 Volume 10		

War Diary	Near Anneux	01/10/1918	04/10/1918
War Diary	Near Moeuvres	05/11/1918	07/11/1918
War Diary	Near Anneux	08/10/1918	08/10/1918
War Diary	Mt Sur Loeuf	09/10/1918	09/10/1918
War Diary	Niergnies	10/10/1918	10/10/1918
War Diary	La. Bahote	11/10/1918	11/10/1918
War Diary	Near Rieux	12/10/1918	16/10/1918
War Diary	Proville	17/10/1918	18/10/1918
War Diary	Lebucquiere	19/10/1918	19/10/1918
War Diary	Fremicourt	20/10/1918	20/10/1918
War Diary	St Eloi	21/10/1918	23/10/1918
War Diary	Courcelles Lez Lens	24/10/1918	25/10/1918
War Diary	Frais Marais	26/10/1918	31/10/1918
Heading	War Diary Of 52nd Divisional Ammunition Column From 1-11-18 To 30-11-18 Volume II		
War Diary	Frais Marais	01/11/1918	02/11/1918
War Diary	Rosult	03/11/1918	08/11/1918
War Diary	Haute Rive	09/11/1918	09/11/1918
War Diary	Peruwelz	10/11/1918	10/11/1918
War Diary	Sirault	11/11/1918	28/11/1918
War Diary	Masnuy St Pierre	29/11/1918	30/11/1918
Heading	War Diary Of 52nd Divisional Ammunition Column From December 1st 1918 To December 31st 1918 Volume XII		
War Diary	Brulotte	01/12/1918	31/12/1918
Heading	War Diary Of 52nd Divisional Ammunition Column From 1-1-19 To 31-1-19 Volume I		
War Diary	Brulotte	01/01/1919	05/01/1919
War Diary	Havre	06/01/1919	31/01/1919
Heading	War Diary Of 52nd Divisional Ammunition Column From 1-2-19 To 28-2-19 Volume II		
War Diary	Havre	01/02/1919	28/02/1919
Heading	War Diary Of 52nd Divisional Ammunition Column From 1-3-19 To 31-3-19 Volume III		
War Diary	Havre	01/03/1919	18/03/1919
War Diary	Soignies	19/03/1919	31/03/1919
Heading	War Diary Of 52nd Divisional Ammunition Column From 1-4-19 To 30-4-19 Volume IV		
War Diary	Soignies	01/04/1919	30/04/1919
Heading	War Diary Of 52nd Divisional Ammunition Column From 1-5-19 To 31-5-19 Volume V		
War Diary			
War Diary	Soignies	01/05/1919	01/05/1919
War Diary	Belgium	09/05/1919	31/05/1919

WO95/2892/5

Dunarenal Ammunition
Company

52ND DIVISION

52ND DIVL AMMUNITION COL.
APR 1918 - MAY 1919

52ND DIVISION

52nd Divisional Artillery

Disembarked MARSEILLES from EGYPT 12.4.18.

52nd DIVISIONAL AMMUNITION COLUMN R.F.A.

APRIL 1918.

APRIL 1918

52nd Divisional Ammunition Column

WAR DIARY

INTELLIGENCE SUMMARY.

Army Form C. 2118.

Place	Date	Hour	Summary of Events and Information	Remarks and references to Appendices
MOASCAR	1.4.18		Orders received for D.A.C. to move on 2nd inst. Reorganization into 3 Sections to be carried out at once. Accordingly No 3 Section was absorbed in No 1 and 2 Sections and B Echelon; A/Capt ALBAN E.C.H taking over command of the latter. The new establishment (Part VIII) gives a total of 71 all ranks including attached and 892 animals; HQ consisting of 36 all ranks with 39 animals; "A" Echelon (1+2 Sections) each 217 all ranks with 270 animals, and B Echelon 239 all ranks with 309 animals. Orders were received to retain 143 Indian drivers with a proportion of NCOs.	AR
— " —	2.4.18		The reorganised DAC moved to MOASCAR STATION, and entrained during the evening after handing in ALL horses, harness, and waggons (except ammunition waggons) to remounts and Ordnance respectively. The train moved off at 2400.	AR
ALEXANDRIA	3.4.18		Arrived ALEXANDRIA 0730. No 1 Section (215 OR) plus 28 OR of B Echelon entrained on HMT "KINGSTONIAN". HQ, No 2 Section, and B Echelon totalling 11 Officers, 3 WOs, 334 BOR, 159 Indians entrained on HMT "MANITOU". Ship moved out of dock at 1600 hrs and remained in harbour for the night. Ships Routine Orders were issued.	AR
AT SEA	4.4.18		Practice Boat Stations carried out. Ship sailed at 1600 hrs.	AR
— " —	5.4.18		At sea	AR

Army Form C. 2118.

WAR DIARY
or
INTELLIGENCE SUMMARY.
(Erase heading not required.)

Instructions regarding War Diaries and Intelligence Summaries are contained in F. S. Regs., Part II. and the Staff Manual respectively. Title pages will be prepared in manuscript.

Place	Date	Hour	Summary of Events and Information	Remarks and references to Appendices
AT SEA	6.4.18		At sea. Gas drill carried out.	AR
"	7.4.18		"	AR
"	8.4.18		"	AR
"	9.4.18		"	AR
"	10.4.18		"WARWICKSHIRE" torpedoed 0615	AR
"	11.4.18		"KINGSTONIAN" torpedoed 0500	AR
MARSEILLES	12.4.18		Arrived MARSEILLES 0830. Disembarkation commenced at once. No 1 Section ex "KINGSTONIAN" less 3 men unaccounted for landed at 0630. At 1700 DAC proceeded to No 8 Rest Camp. Nomenclature of unit becomes "52nd D.A.C." went to Camp FOURNIER.	AR
"	13.4.18		DAC, plus 3 Officers and 33 OR of 133 and 134 T.M. B.Coys, entrained at ARENC station. Train left at 1730.	AR
TRAIN	14.4.18		Travelling all day. Arrived Les Laumes at 1900.	AR
"	15.4.18		Arrived JUVISY 0630. Halted near US about 1100, and remained there until 1700.	AR
NOYELLES	16.4.18		Arrived ABANCOURT at 1100, and ABBEVILLE at 1800. Reached NOYELLES about 1900 and detrained. Unit went to Rest Camp for the night.	AR
PORT LE GRAND	17.4.18		Moved into billet at PORT LE GRAND at 0830. HQ DAC in chateau near village. Stores etc were brought out by motor lorry.	AR

Army Form C. 2118.

WAR DIARY
or
INTELLIGENCE SUMMARY.
(Erase heading not required.)

Instructions regarding War Diaries and Intelligence Summaries are contained in F.S. Regs., Part II. and the Staff Manual respectively. Title pages will be prepared in manuscript.

Place	Date	Hour	Summary of Events and Information	Remarks and references to Appendices
PORT LE GRAND	18.4.18		Drew 316 mules, 3 Watr. Carts, 1 Cart Maltese, 52 Waggons G.S., 15 Waggon Lgd., 70 Double Sets White Harness, 87 Double Sets Lead Harness & 1 Double set Shaft draught Harness. This was all drawn from the form of "complete turnouts".	RS RS RS
"	19.4.18		Nil	RS
"	20.4.18		Clothing, harness etc drawn from Ordnance	RS
"	21.4.18		Capt J. RAMSAY returned from leave & took over command of 'B' Sub-section. 2/Lt H HADLEY transferred to 'attached 'B' Sub-section. Four hundred and eight Remounts drawn from ABBEVILLE	RS RS RS
"	22.4.18		Nil	RS
"	23.4.18		Lt THUAU, French Interpreter reported (on attachment) to HQ	RS
"	24.4.18		Orders received that unit is to be prepared to move on 28th inst. S.A.A. Gun ammunition	RS
"	25.4.18		Date of moving altered, fixed definitely for 27th inst. SAIGNEVILLE.	RS
"	26.4.18		Divn. Goo Office reported and Gas Course for N.C.Os. commenced. No.1 Section received their Amm Waggons. Gas Course continued. No.2 Section filled their amm & waggons.	RS
"	27.4.18		Orders received to move on 27th inst to FROHEN LE PETIT. Train waggons reported. D.A.C. moved to BEAUMONT RIVIERE, marching at 0900. All units were in billets by 1930. No.2 Section	RS
"	28.4.18		D.H.Q. moved from BEAUMONT RIVIÈRE to WILLEMAN. No.2 Section to FRESNOY. Units arrived in billets about 1600.	RS
"	29.4.18			RS
"	30.4.18		D.A.C. moved from WILLEMAN and FRESNOY to EMBRY. Arrived in billets by 1400. At EMBRY	RS

1.5.18.

[signature]
Lt Col D.A.C.

Confidential

Original
No 2

War Diary
of
52nd Divisional Ammn Coln.

from
1.5.1918
to
31.5.18

Vol. III

52nd Div Amm. Column.
WAR DIARY
MAY 1918
INTELLIGENCE SUMMARY.
Army Form C. 2118.

Place	Date	Hour	Summary of Events and Information	Remarks and references to Appendices
EMBRY	1.5.18		Orders received for DAC to move to CREQUY tomorrow at that	AP
CREQUY	2.5.18		DAC moved to CREQUY at 0930.	AP
"	3.5.18		At CREQUY.	AP
"	4.5.18		Two Corporals and 18 gunners transferred to 9th TAB 4.	AP
"	5.5.18		HQ DAC inspected into billet arranged previously by HQ RA. Orders received for SAA & to march tomorrow 6th inst to join 52nd Div near NEUVILLE ST VAAST. Lieut ALBAN admitted to hospital	AP
"	6.5.18		SAA & marched at 0900. Officers and O.R. returned from Course at Reserve Army Artillery School	AP
"	7.5.18		Orders received for D.A.C. to march on 8th inst to ANVIN area	AP
SAUTRECOURT	8.5.18		D.A.C. marched at 0810 and went into billets (HQ at SAUTREVILLE, No 1 & 2 Sections at FLEURY.) Semi-Limbs ROSE.C.B.D and COL. YER MD. & mfriers and were attached to No 1 & 2 Sections respectively	AP
"	9.5.18		At SAUTRECOURT	AP
"	10.5.18		Nil	AP
"	11.5.18		Leave to England opened. Approximate allotment 2 per diem.	AP
"	12.5.18		Lieut Col HOPE & 2 Officers expected from Nos 1 & 2 Sections proceeded up the line for 4 days attachment to units in the Line.	AP
"	13.5.18		Gas Officer from 1st Army inspected Box Respirators	AP
"	14.5.18		Orders received to move to MONCHY BRETON area	AP
MAGNICOURT	15.5.18		Moved to MAGNICOURT at 0900.	AP
ESTREE CAUCHIE	16.5.18		Moved from MAGNICOURT to ESTREE CAUCHIE. Lt Col HOPE returned from Course, also 2 19th Lt Officers.	AP
"	17.5.18		Lt Col J.N. HOPE left to take over command of the 38th Army Bde R.F.A. Capt J RANSOM acting capt T. MAGNAY and O 52nd DAC. Capt L WAKEFORD transferred to command PAASRe from this date. Lieut E.C.H. ALBAN appointed to command No 2 Section, vice Capt L WAKEFORD on from date of rejoining. Remaining 2 officers rejoined from course. Four more can T.	AP
"	18.5.18		CRA inspected time fuses	AP
"	19.5.18		Lieut Col. H. SOWLER left to join 9th YA Bde.	AP

52nd Div'l Amm Column

WAR DIARY
or
INTELLIGENCE SUMMARY
(Erase heading not required.)

Army Form C. 2118.

Instructions regarding War Diaries and Intelligence Summaries are contained in F. S. Regs., Part II. and the Staff Manual respectively. Title pages will be prepared in manuscript.

Place	Date	Hour	Summary of Events and Information	Remarks and references to Appendices
ESTREE CAUCHIE	20.5.18		NIL	
-"-	21.5.18		Two 6 Striking reported going out continuing attacking and going inst 20/24 DA	
-"-	22.5.18		DCS SAAS reported having gun & amm 250 rnds & 8730 shells intermittent 8,000 rpm its SAA in accordance with SC A1019 from Lieut C.J. Bowman attached to HQ RA on taking over duties of RAGO	
VILLERS AU BOIS	23.5.18		DAC less SAAS moved at 1315 to VILLERS AU BOIS. Six hundred rounds 18x ammo up to 527 BS.	
-"-	24.5.18		CRA inspected the lines. Four hundred rounds sent up to 527 BS	
-"-	25.5.18		Lieut ANDREWS and 2Lts proceeded to "Indian Course at ROUEN. Two hundred fifty rounds 18x to 527 BS.	
-"-	26.5.18		Nil	
-"-	27.5.18		2Lt COOK proceeded on course at 1st Army Artillery School. VILLERS AU BOIS shelled intermittently throughout the day.	
-"-	28.5.18		2nd Lieut DANCEY proceeded on leave. 2/Lt DOY returned from leave.	
-"-	29.5.18		Nothing to report.	
-"-	30.5.18		Personnel of HQ and all Sections smelt mustard gas. More intermittent shelling of VILLERS AU BOIS	
-"-	31.5.18		Rev R.P. ROWAN reported and was attached to HQ 52 DAC. Intermittent shelling continued	

J. Kennedy
Capt. Cmdg
52nd D.A.C.
1.6.18

CONFIDENTIAL

WAR DIARY

OF

52nd Div Amm Col.

from 1. June 1918 to 30 June 1918

VOLUME 4

52nd Div Amm Col

WAR DIARY
INTELLIGENCE SUMMARY

Army Form C. 2118.

Place	Date	Hour	Summary of Events and Information	Remarks and references to Appendices
VILLERS AU BOIS	1.6.18		Orders received from HQ RA that DAC (less SAA S) would move to MT ST ELOI on 2nd inst	
-"-	2nd		Preparations made to move to ST ELOI, billets allotted, but order to move were subsequently cancelled. Orders received to move to ST ELOI tomorrow, 4th inst	
-"-	3rd			
-"-	4th		DAC (less SAAS) moved from VILLERS AU BOIS to MT ST ELOI	
MT ST ELOI	5th		Lieut DOUGLAS returned from 14 days leave in U.K. Capt WAKEFORD proceeded on same.	
-"-	6th		All ranks put through gas drill by D.A.G.O	
-"-	7th		A.D.V.S. inspected lines	
-"-	8th		Nil	
-"-	9th		Six rounds from enemy gun fell in proximity to billets. No' Sutton killed. No 111905. Dvr SCALES. J. Wounded " 33048 " LAMBERT N. " 97441 " HARPER. J. " 15884 " MILLER R. Remained at duty " 26897 " DUMPHY. J " 78934 Gnr TAYLOR D.	
-"-	10th		} Nil	
-"-	11th			
-"-	12th			
-"-	13th			

Army Form C. 2118.

52. Div Amm Col
WAR DIARY
or
INTELLIGENCE SUMMARY.
(Erase heading not required.)

Place	Date	Hour	Summary of Events and Information	Remarks and references to Appendices
MT ST ELOI	14th		Capt B.O ELLIS proceeded on 14 days leave to U.K.	B.
—''—	15th		nil	
—''—	16th		Inspection of DAC by BG RA Corps took place at 10.30.	B.
—''—	17th		2/Lt J.D. DONNER posted to DAC and attached for duty to No 1 Sec.	B.
—''—	17th		Lieut BELLAIRS. H.A. admitted to Hospital	B.
—''—	18th		Indian personnel inspected by Lieut Genl. Sir E. LOCKE ELLIOTT	B.
—''—	19th		Capt L. WAKEFORD returned from 14 days leave in U.K.	B.
—''—	20th		nil	
—''—	21st		34 mules and 19 drivers sent to Base Remount Depot on return. Ammunition Waggon team from 6 horse to 4 horse. Spare drivers to spare animals increased from 40 to 64, animal strength in No 1 + 2 Sections increased from 20 to 32.	B.
—''—	22nd		nil	
—''—	23rd		2/Lt HADLEY. proceeded on 14 days leave to U.K.	B.
—''—	24th		Lieut DAVIES proceeded on 14 days leave to U.K.	B.
—''—	25th		nil	
—''—	26th		nil	
—''—	27th		CRA inspected horse lines	B.
—''—	28th		nil	
—''—	29th		nil	
—''—	30		nil	

Signed,
MAJOR. RFA
CMDNG 52 DAC

CONFIDENTIAL

WAR DIARY

OF

52nd DIVISIONAL AMMUNITION COLUMN

from 1-7-18   to 31-7-18

(VOLUMN VII)

52nd Div. Amm Col

Army Form C. 2118.

WAR DIARY
July or 1918
INTELLIGENCE SUMMARY.
(Erase heading not required.)

Place	Date	Hour	Summary of Events and Information	Remarks and references to Appendices
Mt ST ELOI	1.7.18		Nil	
	2 -"-		Capt B.O. Ellis returned from leave in UK	
	3 -"-		Nil	
	4 -"-		-"-	
	5 -"-		Signalling Class commenced under 2/Lt COLLIER.	
	6 -"-		Corps Commander inspected SAA Sect. 2/Lt COLLIER proceeded on leave to PARIS	
	7 -"-		Interpreter DECOMIS reported for duty.	
	8 -"-		Nil	
	9 -"-		2/Lt HADLEY returned from leave in UK	
	10 -"-			
	11 -"-		Nil	
	12 -"-			
	13 -"-			
	14 -"-		Lieut DOUGLAS took over from 2/Lt DOY at TARGETTE DUMP.	
	15 -"-		Interpreter DECOMIS left DAC	
	16 -"-			
	17 -"-			
	18 -"-		2/Lt COLLIER returned from leave in PARIS. 2/Lt R.F. PAGNAM, 2/Lt G.P. WEBB, 2/Lt R. HORSWICK reported for duty. (+ posted to No 1 Sect) (+ to No 2 Sect).	
	19 -"-		Warning order that DIV. ARTY is moving	
	20 -"-		Detailed Orders re move received. Advance Parties from 8th DAC arrived to take over.	
OURTON	21 -"-		52 DAC moved at 1400 to OURTON. Relief by 8th DAC completed. Capt KERMACK proceeded on leave to UK.	

Army Form C. 2118.

52 DAC
WAR DIARY
JULY OF 1918
INTELLIGENCE SUMMARY.
(Erase heading not required.)

Place	Date	Hour	Summary of Events and Information	Remarks and references to Appendices
OURTON	22	-	NIL	AB.
"	23		Capt. J. BOYD joined from 20th Bty, no posted to command No 2 Section	AB.
"	24		Three Officers & 12 O.R. proceeded on T.M. Course. Lieut DAVIES. R.M. returned from leave	AB.
"	25		Nil	AB.
"	26		Q.M.G. Corps Horsemaster inspected lines	AB.
"	27		NIL	AB.
"	28		Warning Order received that Div Arty will probably move South tomorrow	AB.
"	29		Orders received at 0350 for DAC to march to MADAGASCAR Camp near ANZIN	AB. AB.
MADAGASCAR CAMP	30		DAC marched at 0730 via CAMBLAIN L'ABBÉ and arrived in camp at 1500 DAC e took over AUBIN DUMP at 1200	AB. AB.
"	31		Orders received for DAC to march to HABARCQ tomorrow 1st post leaving by 0500. Lieut ANDREWS returned from leave	AB.

J. Gurney. Major R.F.A.
Comdg 52nd DAC

4/8/17

Vol 5

CONFIDENTIAL.
****

ORIGINAL.
=========

WAR DIARY OF 52ND DIVISIONAL AMMUNITION COLUMN.

VOL. VIII.

FROM - 1st AUGUST 1918.   TO - 31st AUGUST 1918.

52nd Div Amm Column

Army Form C. 2118.

WAR DIARY
or
INTELLIGENCE SUMMARY
(Erase heading not required.)

Place	Date	Hour	Summary of Events and Information	Remarks and references to Appendices
HABARCQ	1-8-18	—	DAC moved fm MADAGASCAR to HABARCQ at 0400. Orders received at 1900 for DAC to move to camp at MARŒUIL tomorrow 2nd inst.	AD
MARŒUIL	2-"-	—	DAC moved from HABARCQ to camp near MARŒUIL as follows:- HQ & SAA Sect (S/C) F20d4,2, No1 Sect F20b,3,9, No2 Sect F20d3,4. Arrived about 0930	AD
"	3-"-	—	Nil	AP
"	4-"-	—	DAC commenced drawing Supplies for D.A. units from Refilling Point, Mt S18b01/S5, to Div't Troops Dump	AP
"	5-"-	—	Nil	AP
"	6-"-	—	No	AP
"	7-"-	—	Capt DL CHARLTON shot himself, dried shortly afterwards from his injuries	AP
"	8-"-	—	Capt A.J. KERWICK returned from leave	AP
"	9-"-	—	H.M. The King passed by the Camp, Troops attend to.	AP
"	10-"-	—	2/Lt COOK & Lt DAVIES attached 92/BAC	AP
"	11-"-	—	Nil	
"	12-"-	—	Nil	
"	13-"-	—	Warning Orders for DAC to be prepared to move.	
"	14-"-	—	Orders received for DAC to move to FREVIN CAPELLE tomorrow 15th inst. Order cancelled at 2015. Proportion of AX in echelon raised to 50%, until 50% AX 108 Foot.	AP
FREVIN CAPELLE	15-"-	—	Orders received at 12 noon for DAC to move to FREVIN CAPELLE. Unit moved during the afternoon to location in FREVIN CAPELLE as follows:- HQ, No 1/2 Section E10 & AA (S/C). SAA Sect E9a3.2	AP
"	16-"-	—	Nil	
"	17-"-	—	Orders received for HQ, No1 & No2 Section to be prepared to move to neighbourhood of AUBIN in the afternoon. These orders were subsequently cancelled.	AP
"	18-"-	—	Unit still ordered to be in readiness to move — do —	AP
"	19-"-	—	— do —	AP
"	20-"-	—	DAC Orders to be in readiness to move at night, but orders received later to that effect. Capt ROWAN and 2/Lt DONNER admitted to hospital	AP

PTO

WAR DIARY or INTELLIGENCE SUMMARY

Army Form C. 2118.

52 DAC

Place	Date	Hour	Summary of Events and Information	Remarks and references to Appendices
MONCHIET	21.8.16	—	Orders received at 1500 for DAC to move tonight. Detailed orders received at 1745 to move to BEAUMETZ - MONCHIET area. HQ moved off at 2215 followed by Nos 1, 2 & SAA Sect. Arrival MONCHIET at 0130. Hostile bombing activity considerable.	R.P.
GROSVILLE	22..	—	At 1500 verbal instructions received that DAC will march tonight to camp in area R 20.21, marching at 2000, Nos 1 & 2 Section going direct to B.5 positions and bumping echelon returning to R.P. (TAUNTON DUMP), picking up their own ammunition to carry already earmarked by advance parties (in R 20.21). Orders were received at 1835 for SMS to march direct to new camping area. HQ & SMS to march direct to new camping area. HQ & SMS to deliver SAA & grenades to the infantry, waggons were sent off at 1945 to dump as referred to. Filling grenades reported. At 2000 Nos 1 & 2 Sections were referred to filling grenades reported. G.S. waggons & Nos 1 & 2 Sections not being used for ammn 3 empty. Arrived in camp at 0100, units having been much delayed by the congestion on the roads. HQ arrived at (SIC) R 20 & 5.6 with No 2 Sect., No 1 at R 20 & 7.6. SMS at R 20 c 4.6. Waggons returned from Ammn Supply having refilled No 1 at 0630. No 2 at 0715. SMS were in load to move to R67 & 3.3 at 0630 & moving and ammn. dump at D.W.2. At 1830 Nos 1 & 2 Section proceeded to B.5 Position and dumped 100 Rds per gun next How.	R.P.
" "	23..		At 0345 40 R.A. Order No 155 received ordering DAC to move all ammn 3 in echelon at new B.5 positions (amour). Fill up on return journey. Sections moved off at about 0630 still not return until about 1600. 2/Lt DOWNTHWAITE and 2/Lt BICKMORE posted to D.A.C. Britain supplied and ammunition as called for.	R.P.
" "	24..			R.
" "	25..			R.P.
" "	26..		Ammunition and minor arms parts supplied to Batteries.	R.
" "	27..		Orders received at 0330 for DAC to move to area S4 & c6 at 0630. Nos 1 & 2 Sections and HQ moved off accordingly, went into camp at M33 & Q0 (S.1.S.) Ammunition supply up to noon heavy, afternoon normal.	R.P.

Army Form C. 2118.

WAR DIARY
or
INTELLIGENCE SUMMARY.
(Erase heading not required.)

52 DAC

Place	Date	Hour	Summary of Events and Information	Remarks and references to Appendices
N.R. MERICOURT	28.8.18		Ammunition Supply normal	App
	29.8.18		Ammunition Supply heavy. 2/Lt DAVIES & 2/Lt COOK struck off strength of DAC posted to 9th Bde RFA as from 9th inst.	App
	30 " "		Ammunition Supply heavy	App
	31 " "		do	App

J. Savant
Major RFA
Cmdt 52 DAC

1.9.18

Vol 6

= CONFIDENTIAL =

WAR - DIARY.

OF

52nd Divisional Ammunition Column.

From 1-9-1918   To 30-9-1918.

(VOLUME IX)

[ORIGINAL]

Army Form C. 2118.

WAR DIARY
OF 52nd DIV Amm Column
INTELLIGENCE SUMMARY.
(Erase heading not required.)

Instructions regarding War Diaries and Intelligence Summaries are contained in F. S. Rgns., Part II. and the Staff Manual respectively. Title pages will be prepared in manuscript.

Place	Date	Hour	Summary of Events and Information	Remarks and references to Appendices
NEAR MERCATEL	1.9.18		Ammunition Supply normal. At 1530 orders received for 700 rounds per gun & 550 rounds per How to be dumped at BFY K/Line. This amount was subsequently reduced to 300 rounds per 18 Pdr and 200 rounds per How. The dumping was completed before 0500 2nd inst.	
NEAR HENIN	2.9.18		Orders received with orders from HQ for DAC to move to area T9 on 2nd inst. Lieut Rowan rejoined from hospital. 2/Lt SOUTHWAITE struck off the strength. DAC (less SAAS) moved forward into camp at T3.d.9.3. At 1900 two others were received to move to vicinity of FONTAINE LES CROISILLES. In the darkness a camping ground could not be found so units bivouaced about 76 C.	
NEAR CAGNICOURT	3.9.18		HQ No 1 No 2 Sect moved into camp at O 32 d O 3. At 1235 orders were received to move to vicinity of CULLING CURD COPSE in V 13. (S/B) (near FONTAINE LEZ CROISILLES) Units moved at 14/5. Ammunition supply normal.	
— " —	4.9.18		Ammunition Supply heavy	
— " —	5 "		" " normal	
— " —	6 "		" " "	
— " —	7 "		" " normal. Lt Bowman rejoined from leave in UK	
— " —	8 "		" " normal	
NEAR CROISILLES	9 "		" " small	
— " —	10 "		Orders received for DAC (less SAAS) to move to area V 19. Moved accordingly at 1400 to V19 & 8.9	
— " —	11 "		NIL	
— " —	12 "		T M Btty moved into camp in vicinity of DAC. Ammunition Supply heavy	
— " —	13 "		Nil	
— " —	14 "		2/Lt DONNER returned from hospital	
— " —	15 "		Shell exploded in lines at about 2130 killing 14 mules, and wounding 23 other animals. Dr O R was slightly wounded.	
— " —	16 "		Heavy storm night 16/17 18	
— " —	17 "		Nil	
— " —	18 "		Amm. Supply heavy night 17/18	

Army Form C. 2118.

WAR DIARY
52nd (or?) DIV AMM COLUMN
INTELLIGENCE SUMMARY.
(Erase heading not required.)

Instructions regarding War Diaries and Intelligence Summaries are contained in F. S. Regs., Part II. and the Staff Manual respectively. Title pages will be prepared in manuscript.

Place	Date	Hour	Summary of Events and Information	Remarks and references to Appendices
NEAR CROISILLES	19		During night 18/19 about 12 HV shells fell in camp of DAC without causing damage	
" "	20		Fourteen trained TM personnel sent up as reinforcements to DTMO – also 20 reinforcements as ammunition carriers	
" "	21		Warning order that DAC (less SAA Sect) will move to LAGNICOURT area	
NEAR LAGNICOURT	22		Moved to C.21.d.9.2. (West of LAGNICOURT) at 13.30. 200 rounds A per gun, & 204 rounds Bx per How sent up to 9th Bde positions	
" "	23		Nil	
" "	24		Orders on "Z" day received	
" "	25			
" "	26		Orders received for DAC (less SAA) to move at Zero + 90 minutes on "Z" day (27.9.18) to LOUVERVAL.	
LOUVERVAL	27		52nd DAC moved at 0650 to LOUVERVAL (JH t 64.57c), remained there all day. Ammunition supply moderate.	
NEAR MOEUVRES	28		DAC (less SAAS) moved at 0830 to J.21.C.2.8. Amm Supply moderate. At 2000 Ohrs were received to move to L.2.a. (E of GRAINCOURT). DAC moved at 21.15. On arrival at L2.a. orders received to camp Sugar Factory (L29a), but no suitable camping ground could be found there. Units returned to get camping ground on J.21.c.	
NEAR GRAINCOURT	29		Orders received to move to L.2.a. wherenits moved independently at 15.30.	
	30		Quiet day, Ammunition supply small	

[signature]
Major RFA
Cmdr 52 DAC

1/4/18

CONFIDENTIAL.

War Diary

OF

52nd Divisional Ammunition Column

From: 1-10-18   To: 31-10-18

Volume - 10

1-31 OCTOBER 1918

Army Form C. 2118.

WAR DIARY
52nd Divl Ammunition Column
INTELLIGENCE-SUMMARY

(Erase heading not required.)

Instructions regarding War Diaries and Intelligence Summaries are contained in F. S. Regs., Part II. and the Staff Manual respectively. Title pages will be prepared in manuscript.

Place	Date	Hour	Summary of Events and Information	Remarks and references to Appendices
NEAR ANNEUX	1.10.18	—	Amn & Supply movents. Dumped echelon at Btys w/Lines in the evening & refilled.	
	2 —"—	—	Dumped echelon in Bty w/Lines and refilled.	
	3 —"—	—	nil	
	4 —"—	—	nil	
NEAR MOEUVRES	5 —"—	—	2/Lt W.B. COLLIER transferred to 56 Bde RFA. 52 DAC (less Staff Sect) moved at 1400 to camp at E 24 d 8.0 (near MOEUVRES). At 2330 orders received to send up 200 Rds A per gun to 9th Bde w/Lines. This was done	
"	6 —"—	—	5th Bty. A per gun to send up 200 Rds A per gun to 56 Bde. Winter Zero came into force midnight 5th/6th	
"	7 —"—	—	Orders received to dump 100 rds 18 Pr per gun at 9th & 56th Bdes W/Lines. This was done. Salvage of 6 German guns carried out.	
NEAR ANNEUX	8 —"—	—	DAC moved at 1000 to L 2 a (near ANNEUX). Amn & Supply & supply of spare parts heavy	
MT SUR L'OEUF	9 —"—	—	Moved at 1300 to G 8 c 8.1 (MT SUR L'OEUF). Amn & Supply moderate	
NIERGNIES	10 —"—	—	Moved at noon to G 11 a 9.9 (W of NIERGNIES). Amn & Supply moderate.	
LA BAHOTE	11 —"—	—	Moved at 1300 to B 10 a 5.5 (LA BAHOTE). Amn & Supply in the evening heavy	
NEAR RIEUX	12 —"—	—	Moved at 1300 to C 2 c 5.5. (near RIEUX). Amn & Supply heavy	
—"—	13 —"—	—	nil	
—"—	14 —"—	—	Amn & Supply normal	
—"—	15 —"—	—	nil	
—"—	16 —"—	—	Weather very wet	
PROVILLE	17 —"—	—	52 DAC (less Staff) moved to F 30 a 4.5 (nr PROVILLE). Ten GOW waggons turned in to bty.	
—"—	18 —"—	—	NIL	

D. D. & L., London, E.C.
(A3-94) Wt W1777/M2091 750,000 5/17 Sch. 52 Forms/C2118/14

Army Form C. 2118.

WAR DIARY
or
INTELLIGENCE SUMMARY.
(Erase heading not required.)

Page II

Place	Date	Hour	Summary of Events and Information	Remarks and references to Appendices
LEBUCQUIERE FREMICOURT	19		Moved to LEBUCQUIERE (I24 c 6.0 Sheet 57c) 52 DAC (less SAA Sect) entrained at VELU (Not Sect) + proceeded by rail to ECURIE & ACQ respectively. HQ Mo2 filliled in ST ELOI. Not at ECURIE	
ST ELOI	20		At ST ELOI	
"	21		Units bathing, refitting. No.1 Sect moved from ECURIE to ST ELOI	
"	22		Nil	
	23		DAC (less SAA Sect) moved from ST ELOI to COURCELLES LEZ LENS	
COURCELLES LEZ LENS	24		At COURCELLES	
	25		52 DAC (less SAA Sect) moved from COURCELLES to FRAIS MARAIS (Sheet 44A X.1)	
FRAIS MARAIS	26		Nil	
"	27		Nil	
"	28		CRA inspected lines of No.1 Mo.2 Sects	
"	29		Nil	
"	30		Lieut ROSE Lieut DOY attached 56th Bde. Major RAMSAY went on leave	
	31			

M Miller Capt RFA
for Major Comdg
1.11.18
52 DAC

Vol 8

CONFIDENTIAL

WAR DIARY

of

52nd Divisional Ammunition Column

From 1-11-18 To 30-11-18

Volume 11

Army Form C. 2118.

52nd D.A.C. Ammn Column

WAR DIARY
or
INTELLIGENCE SUMMARY.
(Erase heading not required.)

Instructions regarding War Diaries and Intelligence Summaries are contained in F. S. Regs., Part II and the Staff Manual respectively. Title pages will be prepared in manuscript.

Place	Date	Hour	Summary of Events and Information	Remarks and references to Appendices
FRAIS MARAIS	1/11/18	-	No 2 Section moved to H12d (Sheet 44), West of RUMEGIES	
"	2-11-		nil	
ROSULT	3-11-		2/Lt H. PARKER posted to 52 D.A.C. HQ No1 Section moved to ROSULT from FRAIS MARAIS	
"	4-11-		nil	
"	5-11-		nil	
"	6-11-		No 2 Section moved to ROSULT. Lieut C.T. BOWMAN & hospital	
"	7-11-		2/Lt H.I. BINNS reported for duty	
"	8-11-		Lieut H.A. BELLAIRS reported for duty	
HAUTE RIVE	9-11-		DAC (less SAA Sect) moved at 0630 to CHAUSSEE. Orders received to move on to HAUTE RIVE at noon. Units arrived in camp about 1600	
PERUWELZ	10-11-		Orders to move to PERUWELZ. Arrived at 1600	
SIRAULT	11-11-		Orders received that hostilities cease at 1100. DAC (less SAA Sect) moved to SIRAULT. Lieut DOUGLAS went on leave	
"	12- "	⎫		
"	13- "		nil	
"	14- "			
"	15- "			
"	16- "	⎭		
"	17- "	⎫	Divl Thanksgiving Service. Major J. RAM sat returned from leave	
"	18- "			
"	19- "		nil	
"	20- "	⎭		

Army Form C. 2118.

WAR DIARY
or
INTELLIGENCE SUMMARY.
(Erase heading not required.)

Instructions regarding War Diaries and Intelligence Summaries are contained in F. S. Regs., Part II. and the Staff Manual respectively. Title pages will be prepared in manuscript.

Place	Date	Hour	Summary of Events and Information	Remarks and references to Appendices
SIRAULT	21		Lieut E.S. WISE, 2/Lt R. SHAW, 2/Lt R.T. HADDON reported for duty	
"	22		Nil	
"	23		Capt T. BOYD proceeded on leave	
"	24		2/Lt W.A. GREENSLADE reported for duty	
"	25		Nil	
"	26		-"-	
"	27		-"-	
"	28		-"-	
"	29		52 DAC moved from SIRAULT to CASTEAU area. Capt WAKEFORD went on leave, Lieut F. DOUGLAS returned from leave	
MASNUY ST PIERRE	30		Nil	

J. Lunsent
Major RFA
Cmdg 52 DAC

1-12-18

CONFIDENTIAL

War Diary

of

52nd Divisional Ammunition Column

Volume XII

From December 1st 1918   To December 31st 1918

Army Form C. 2118.

WAR DIARY
52nd Div: Amm: Column.
INTELLIGENCE SUMMARY.

(Erase heading not required.)

Instructions regarding War Diaries and Intelligence
Summaries are contained in F. S. Regs., Part II.
and the Staff Manual respectively. Title pages
will be prepared in manuscript.

Place	Date	Hour	Summary of Events and Information	Remarks and references to Appendices
BRULOTTE	1.12.18		Nil	
"	2 "		"	
"	3 "		"	
"	4 "		2/Lt H. HADLEY went on leave	
"	5 "		Nil	
"	6 "		2/Lt R. SHAW went on T.M Course	
"	7 "		Capt B.O. ELLIS went on leave	
"	8 "		Nil	
"	9 "		Nil	
"	10 "		Nil	
"	11 "		Capt J. BOYD returned from leave	
"	12 "		Nil	
"	13 "		2/Lt H. PARKER went on leave	
"	14 "		C.R.A visited S.A.A. Section	
"	15 "		Nil	
"	16 "		C.R.A visited H.Q, No1 No2 Sections	
"	17 "		Nil	
"	18 "		Nil	
"	19 "		Nil	
"	20 "		Lieut ANDREWS went on leave	
"	21 "		Nil	
"	22 "		Lieut DOY posted to 56 Bde. Lt ROSE returned to DAC from 56 Bde C.V.D	
"	23 "		2/Lt R. SHAW returned from T.M Course	
"	24 "		Nil	
"	25 "		Nil	
"	26 "		Nil	
"	27 "		Lieut C.H. ROTHERA left for Special Leave	

Army Form C. 2118.

WAR DIARY
or
INTELLIGENCE SUMMARY
(Erase heading not required.)

Instructions regarding War Diaries and Intelligence Summaries are contained in F. S. Regs., Part II. and the Staff Manual respectively. Title pages will be prepared in manuscript.

Place	Date	Hour	Summary of Events and Information	Remarks and references to Appendices
BRULOTTE	28		Nil	
"	29		Capt B.O. Ellis returned from leave	
"	30		GOC Div & CRA inspected Nos 1 & 2 Sections	
"	31		First party of Coal Miners for demobilization despatched. 2/Lt R. Shaw conducting Officer	

31.12.18

[signature]
Major RFA
Cmdng 52 D.A.C.

Vol 10

— CONFIDENTIAL —

— WAR — DIARY —

— OF —

— 52ND DIVISIONAL — AMMUNITION — COLUMN —

— FROM 1-1-19 — TO 31-1-19 —

— VOLUME I —

ORIGINAL

Army Form C. 2118.

WAR DIARY
32nd D.A.C. or Ammn. Column
INTELLIGENCE SUMMARY.
(Erase heading not required.)

Instructions regarding War Diaries and Intelligence Summaries are contained in F. S. Regs., Part II. and the Staff Manual respectively. Title pages will be prepared in manuscript.

Place	Date	Hour	Summary of Events and Information	Remarks and references to Appendices
BRULOTTE	1.1.19.		2/Lt H Parker rejoined from leave	
"	2.		2/Lt Prestoure went on leave	
"	3.		2/Lt C.V.D Rose went to hospital	
"	4.		nil	
"	5.		nil	
"	6.		D.A.C. moved H.Q. & No 2 Section to HAVRE: No 1 Sect. to Oborg?	
HAVRE	7.		Capt. W.V.H. BUTLER rejoined from Cinema U.K.	
"	8.		nil	
"	9.		nil	
"	10.		DAC began drawing supplies from Railhead for R.P.	
"	11.		2/Lt Andrews rejoined from leave	
"	12.		2/Lt Dennen (Conducting Officer) left unit	
"	13.		15 A.A. Section moved to St. DENIS.	
"	14.			
"	15.			
"	16.			
"	17.		NIL	
"	18.			
"	19.			
"	20.			
"	21.		2/Lt H.Parker took up duties as Demobilisation Officer and undertify to Rai?	
"	22.		NIL	
"	23.			
"	24.			
"	25.		C R A.D.D. &U./London, E.C. S.B.A. Sapton	

Army Form C. 2118.

WAR DIARY
or
INTELLIGENCE SUMMARY.
(Erase heading not required.)

Instructions regarding War Diaries and Intelligence Summaries are contained in F. S. Regs., Part II. and the Staff Manual respectively. Title pages will be prepared in manuscript.

Place	Date	Hour	Summary of Events and Information	Remarks and references to Appendices
HAVRE	26/1/19		NIL	
"	27			
"	28			
"	29			
"	30			
"	31			

3/2/19.

[signature]
Major R.F.A.
Commanding 52nd B.A.C.

CONFIDENTIAL

WAR — DIARY

OF

52nd DIVISIONAL AMMUNITION COLUMN

FROM 1-2-19 TO 28-2-19

VOLUME II

Army Form C. 2118.

WAR DIARY 52nd Divisional Ammunition Column
or
INTELLIGENCE SUMMARY.

(Erase heading not required.)

February 1919

Instructions regarding War Diaries and Intelligence Summaries are contained in F. S. Regs., Part II. and the Staff Manual respectively. Title pages will be prepared in manuscript.

Place	Date	Hour	Summary of Events and Information	Remarks and references to Appendices
HAVRE	Feb 1	—	Conference at H.Q.R.A. with O.C. H. 18th D.A.C. Lieut. Col. Hadley. Leave waiting for UK on Demobilization. Major Ellis & Lt Hadley	
"	2		52nd Divl Train motors came to cart all remaining personal kits to D.A.C. Also 2 men (N.C.O's) to take charge M Stores etc	
"	3		nil	
"	4		D.A.C. re-arranging rations for D.A. at Godiakald. Regimental fatigues from Jemappes to supply troops at CASTEAU & Jubilee Road (J12A y.3) at Sheet 45.	
"	5		nil	
"	6		D.A. Boundaries MONS	
"	7		nil	
"	8		nil	
"	9		Road fatigue began on B.C. front.	
"	10		nil	
"	11		21 as at GREEDSLADE Heads sent for U.K. for Demobilization	
"	12		nil	
"	13		Col. the Earl of DEMBIGH Lectures at Col. G mess MONS	
"	14		nil	
"	15		500 Ammunition Collecting Point formed at No 1 Sect for all Small Ammunition Post. Supplies issued to D.A.C from (J12 A y.3 Jubilee Road) on which for refill for reinforcements own arrangement	
"	16		Road fatigue recommenced (same as on 3rd)	
"	17		Major Haas recantions received from D.A.H.Q.	
"	18		nil	
"	19		21 MULES sent to 20 Vet Evac Station MONS	
"	20		Lieut HADDON R.T. left unit for draft conducting duties G.R.A. MSik no 2 Section HQ	

Army Form C. 2118.

WAR DIARY
or
INTELLIGENCE SUMMARY.
(Erase heading not required.)

Instructions regarding War Diaries and Intelligence Summaries are contained in F. S. Regs., Part II. and the Staff Manual respectively. Title pages will be prepared in manuscript.

Place	Date	Hour	Summary of Events and Information	Remarks and references to Appendices
HAVRE	Oct. 21.		nil	
	22		4 Y Horses sent to CALAIS (via Remount Staging Camp MONS)	
	23		102 mules entrained at MONS for sale at ROUEN. Indian SBAS held at SABS for 52 DAC.	
	24		6 Y Horses sent to BOULOGNE.	
	25		21 mules sent to SOIGNIES for sale in 28th	
	26		nil	
	27		2 Y animals sent to Remount Staging Camp "MONS"	
	28			
	29			

J. Ramsay
Major S.R.
Commanding 52 DAC.

No 12

CONFIDENTIAL

WAR DIARY

OF

52ND DIVISONAL AMMUNITION COLUMN

VOLUME III.

FROM 1-3-19 TO 31-3-19

HEADQUARTERS,
52ND
DIVL. AMM. COLUMN.

No. ....
Date 2-4-19

Army Form C. 2118.

52ND DIVL. AMM. COLUMN.
No. 19193
Date 1st May 1919

WAR DIARY
or
INTELLIGENCE SUMMARY.
(Erase heading not required.)

Instructions regarding War Diaries and Intelligence Summaries are contained in F. S. Regs., Part II. and the Staff Manual respectively. Title pages will be prepared in manuscript.

Place	Date	Hour	Summary of Events and Information	Remarks and references to Appendices
HAVRE	1.		nil	
	2.		25 Animals/Mules to Base Depot	
	3.		nil	
	4.		1/3 mule to FORGES-LES-EAUX.	
	5.		nil	
	6.		nil	
	7.		Court of Enquiry held re loss of mule from lines of no 1 Section	
	8.			
	9.		Lieut (Capt) R.P. ROWAN left unit for leave to UK	
	10.		nil	
	11.		nil	
	12.		All ammunition cleared from Collecting Point as no 1 Section	
	13.		2/Lt. HADDON rejoined unit from leave	
	14.		1 Y/M Mare to Base	
	15.		3H Z horses to Base	
	16.			
	17.		Billeting parties go to SOIGNIES	
	18.		DAC left HAVRE + moved into SOIGNIES	
SOIGNIES	19.		Lt. MALCOLM joined from 9th Bn.	
	20.		nil	
	21.		234 mules + class entrain at JURBISE, en route for COLOGNE 2nd ARMY. Lt BELLAIR'S conducting	
	22.			
	23.			
	24.		19 AS of _ _ Sent to Base.	

Army Form C. 2118.

WAR DIARY
or
INTELLIGENCE SUMMARY.
(Erase heading not required.)

52ND
DIVL. AMM. COLUMN.
No. 1919/5
Date MARCH 1919

Place	Date	Hour	Summary of Events and Information	Remarks and references to Appendices
SOIGNIES	26/3/19		Nil.	
"	26		2 Squadron under CAPT WAKEFORD and Lt. MALCOLM left with all Indian Personnel for LE HAVRE	
"	27		Lt. E.S. WISE left UNIT for Demob. repatriation.	
"	28		nil.	
"	29		nil.	
"	30		nil	
"	31		Lt. H.A. BELLAIRS left unit for leave to U.K.	

[signature] Major RFA
Commanding 52 D.A.C.

CONFIDENTIAL

WAR DIARY Vol 13

OF

52nd. DIVISIONAL AMMUNITION COLUMN

VOLUME. IV.

FROM 1.4.19. To 30.4.19.

Army Form C. 2118.

WAR DIARY
or
INTELLIGENCE SUMMARY.
(Erase heading not required.)

Instructions regarding War Diaries and Intelligence Summaries are contained in F.S. Regs., Part II. and the Staff Manual respectively. Title pages will be prepared in manuscript.

Place	Date	Hour	Summary of Events and Information	Remarks and references to Appendices
Soignies	April 1		Lt. H.A. BELLAIRS left for UK on Ord Leave.	
"	2		NIL	
"	16			
"	19		Lt. H.A. BELLAIRS rejoined from leave UK.	
"	19		NIL	
"	20		Lt. H.A. BELLAIRS left DAC, posted to Highland DA (Rhine Army)	
"	21		nil	
"	22		Party from DAC visit WATERLOO	
"	23			
"	24		nil	
"	25			
"	26		9 train wagons taken over from 217 Coy R.A.S.C.	
"	27		nil	
"	28		Lt. A. KOLLETT posted from 9 Base RA on June S.A.A.S.	
"	29			
"	30			

Signed,
Major R.T.
Commanding 52 D.A.C.

WD 14

CONFIDENTIAL

WAR DIARY

OF

52nd DIVISIONAL AMMUNITION COLUMN

VOLUME X

From 1-5-19 to 31-9-19.

Army Form C. 2118.

WAR DIARY
or
INTELLIGENCE SUMMARY.
(Erase heading not required.)

Instructions regarding War Diaries and Intelligence Summaries are contained in F. S. Regs., Part II. and the Staff Manual respectively. Title pages will be prepared in manuscript.

Place	Date	Hour	Summary of Events and Information	Remarks and references to Appendices

(A8.09) Wt W3777/M2031 750,000 5/17 **Sch. 52** Forms/C2118/14
D. D. & I., London, E.C.

WAR DIARY May 1919
or
INTELLIGENCE SUMMARY.
(Erase heading not required.)

Army Form C. 2118.

Place	Date	Hour	Summary of Events and Information	Remarks and references to Appendices
Bourges Belgium	1 to 8		NIL	
	9		2/Lt. J. W. COLLETT posted to 9th F.A. Bde	
	10		Capt. H. PARKER left for U.K. for demobilization 2/Lt. R. T. MADDON posted to 147th A.F.A. Bde.	
	11 to 15		NIL	
	16		Lieut. J. H. ANDREWS posted to 147th A.F.A. Bde.	
	17 & 18		NIL	
	19		2/Lt. J. W. TUDD attached to No. 1. Section from 9th F.A. Bde.	
	20		NIL	
	21 to 31		NIL	

[signature]
Major R.F.A.
Commanding 52nd D.A.C.